COBBLESTONE · THE CIVIL WAR

Gettysburg

Bold Battle in the North

Cobblestone Publishing
A Division of Carus Publishing
Peterborough, NH
www.cobblestonepub.com

Staff

Editorial Director: Lou Waryncia

Editor: Sarah Elder Hale

Book Design: David Nelson, www.dnelsondesign.com

Proofreaders: Meg Chorlian, Eileen Terrill

Text Credits

The content of this volume is derived from articles that first appeared in *COBBLESTONE* magazine. Contributors: Rollie Aden, Helen Wieman Bledsoe, Hilda Brucker, Duane Damon, Betty J. Gair, Sarah Elder Hale, Harold Holzer, Heather Mitchell, Janine Richardson, Caryl Simon-Katler.

Picture Credits

Photos.com: 3, 13, 16, 17, 24, 28, 34, 39; Collections of Virginia Historical Society/Center for Virginia History: 4–5; Library of Congress: 6, 15 (top), 19, 26, 31, 32, 33, 38 (top), 41, 42; Clipart.com: 7, 8, 9, 12, 18, 21, 25, 29, 36, 37, 40; Fred Carlson: 10–11; from Henry M. Field, *Blood Is Thicker Than Water: A Few Days Among Our Southern Brethren*, 1886: 14; Gettysburg National Military Park: 10 (inset), 15 (bottom); from *Harper's Weekly* magazine, July 12, 1862: 22; New Hampshire Historical Society: 30. Images for "Civil War Time Line," pages 44–45, courtesy of Photos.com, Clipart.com, and Library of Congress.

Cover

James Walker, *Gettysburg, the First Day*
Courtesy of the West Point Museum, U.S. Military Academy

Library of Congress Cataloging-in-Publication Data

Gettysburg : bold battle in the North / [project director, Lou Waryncia; editor, Sarah Elder Hale].

    p. cm.— (Cobblestone: the Civil War)

    Includes index.

    ISBN 0-8126-7903-2 (hardcover)

    1. Gettysburg, Battle of, Gettysburg, Pa., 1863—Juvenile literature.

    I. Waryncia, Lou. II. Hale, Sarah Elder. III. Series.

    E475.53.G39635 2005

    973.7'349—dc22   2005015215

Printed in China

Cobblestone Publishing

30 Grove Street, Suite C

Peterborough, NH 03458

www.cobblestonepub.com

Table of Contents

Lee's Push North

On May 14, 1863, two years into the bloody Civil War, General Robert E. Lee, commander of the Confederate troops in the East, was on a train to Richmond, Virginia, the Confederate capital. As the train clattered along the

tracks, Lee watched the greening countryside and thought about plans for a possible campaign. He was going to Richmond to meet with the president of the Confederacy, Jefferson Davis.

Lee looked pale, thin, and worried. He fretted because Union troops under General Ulysses S. Grant had surrounded Vicksburg, a Southern fortress that protected the Mississippi River. Grant's troops had stopped the flow of much-needed supplies to the Confederate soldiers there. Other Union troops, under General

Most of the fighting during the Civil War took place in Southern states. Lee's bold move to wage a battle on Northern soil took everyone by surprise.

Joseph Hooker, threatened Richmond. Lee agonized over his plan to turn the Civil War in the South's favor.

In Richmond, Lee met with Davis and explained his plan. The general felt that the South must make a major offensive into Union territory. He hoped this offensive would take the pressure off Richmond, disrupt Federal railroads, get supplies for his troops, and encourage European countries to send a fleet in support of the Confederacy. Davis approved Lee's plan and sent him back to his men.

In failing to stop Lee in Virginia, Union general Joseph Hooker made a critical mistake. A few weeks later, President Abraham Lincoln removed Hooker as commander of the Army of the Potomac.

The Confederates Move North

A few days later, Lee started his army northward, a move that surprised many Union officers. They could not believe that Lee would leave Richmond and head into enemy territory. Hooker ordered his cavalry unit to intercept Lee's troops. In a fierce but inconclusive battle and one of the largest cavalry engagements, the Union riders clashed with General J.E.B. Stuart's Confederate cavalry at Brandy Station, Virginia, on June 9, 1863. But Lee and his army marched on.

Hooker responded cautiously. Earlier in May, Hooker had lost a battle to Lee at Chancellorsville, Virginia, and he did not want to lose another. He allowed the Confederates to advance uncontested, and the South gradually gained the momentum that Lee had hoped for.

The Long, Hot March

Throughout June 1863, thousands of Civil War soldiers marched north from Virginia to Pennsylvania. They trekked 20 to 30 miles a day through the scorching heat. Hiking for hours over dusty, unpaved roads, the soldiers stopped for infrequent meals of pork and dry biscuits. One Confederate soldier wrote in his diary that in a single day he had consumed "breakfast in Virginia, whiskey in Maryland, and supper in Pennsylvania." As the Confederate troops advanced, they defeated a Union force at Winchester, Virginia, and secured the supplies they needed to continue.

Confederate cavalry general J.E.B. Stuart kept the Union forces busy at Brandy Station, Virginia, allowing Lee's army to proceed north.

Keeping the Yankees Guessing

The Union officers, President Abraham Lincoln, and the people of the North overestimated Lee's strength. In reality, Lee had fewer soldiers than the Union army, and his men were poorly equipped. However, fearing an attack, civilians fled to safety, and shopkeepers shipped the goods from their stores to towns farther away. Lincoln especially worried about the safety of Washington, D.C., and Baltimore, Maryland.

As Lee continued to push his army north from Virginia into Pennsylvania, he hoped to draw the Union army away from Richmond, Virginia. Union leaders were not sure exactly where Lee was headed, but John Buford, a general in the Union cavalry, was sent with two brigades (approximately 3,000 men) to Gettysburg, Pennsylvania.

Gettysburg, a quiet farm town just over the Maryland border, lay 70 miles northwest of Washington, D.C., and was located at the intersection of nine major roads. Buford's duty was to hold the town until Union infantry could get there from northern Virginia. Buford and his men rode into Gettysburg around noon on June 30, 1863.

General John Buford took two Union brigades to Gettysburg, Pennsylvania, to guard the intersection of nine major roads.

7

Gettysburg: From Farmland to Battlefield

What did Gettysburg look like in 1863? This was farm country, with rural roads, split-rail and stone fences, barns, and log, frame, stone, and brick houses. Bluebells and hollyhocks bloomed abundantly in the gardens, and the fertile land supported corn, wheat, and peach and apple orchards.

Founded in 1786, the town was named for James Gettys, who had laid out 210 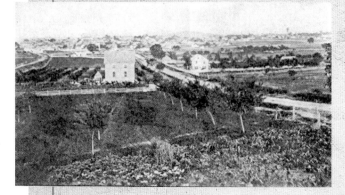 lots on his father's old farm. By the mid-1800s, Gettysburg was home to more than 2,400 inhabitants. Located in a prosperous market region, it featured two colleges: Lutheran Theological Seminary, high on Seminary Ridge, and Pennsylvania College.

Gettysburg was set amid rolling hills, ridges, and valleys. Seminary Ridge lay to the west and Culp's Hill to the southeast. Cemetery Ridge and Little and Big Round Tops framed the shallow valley, which measured two miles from north to south and half a mile wide. It was an ideal spot for 19th-century warfare, which focused on strategic heights and maneuvers.

When the two armies met, they fought in a wheat field and a peach orchard, where the fruit was just beginning to ripen. They also fought in Devil's Den amid a jumble of rocks and trees. Bullets passed within inches of homes, and many civilians fled their burning farms. The remains of the thousands of soldiers who died littered the fields and yards, and the town's colleges, churches, and homes, as well as surrounding farmsteads, were converted into hospitals for the wounded.

He quickly placed troops across McPherson's Ridge, a rolling hill west of town. Buford ordered pickets and vedettes farther west to watch for the advance of the enemy.

As Lee approached Pennsylvania, he realized that the Confederate cavalry led by J.E.B. Stuart had been out of touch for some time. In those days, the horse-mounted cavalry served as the "eyes and ears of the army." (Lee would find out later that Stuart had gone on a mission to ride around the Union forces.) Therefore, Lee was forced to continue north without knowing the exact position, strength, and activities of the Union troops. On June 28, a Confederate spy reported to Lee that he saw Union soldiers camped a few miles east in Frederick, Maryland. Shocked, Lee ordered his troops to come together in Cashtown, Pennsylvania, with the mountains at their back to protect their flanks and rear.

A New Commander

That same day, Lincoln was pondering the situation. Hooker's hesitancy in pursuing Lee had shaken the president's confidence in the general. Lincoln decided to replace him with General George G. Meade. Meade was not widely known to the nation, but he was a reliable officer and had performed well in other battles. Meade intended to make his stand against Lee in Maryland.

Both Meade and Lee knew that they would soon face each other in battle. Meade pushed his army north from Frederick, always conscious that he must protect Washington, D.C., and Baltimore, while Lee's army stayed at Cashtown. On July 1, one of the Confederate generals sent men into Gettysburg, seven miles to the east, to find supplies and shoes for the Southern soldiers. Little did they know that Buford was there with a contingent of Union troops. When Union and Confederate soldiers clashed near Gettysburg, it was coincidence, not strategy, that brought them together.

Key Players

George G. Meade
1815–1872

After graduating from West Point military academy in 1835, George G. Meade spent several years in the South as a military engineer. He served in the U.S.–Mexican War, fighting gallantly at the Battle of Monterrey.

From the start of the Civil War, Meade was a strong leader and rose steadily through the ranks. He was wounded during the Seven Days Campaign but recovered in time to command forces at Second Manassas and South Mountain. At Antietam, Fredericksburg, and Chancellorsville he showed courage and quickness when other officers hesitated. Three days before the Battle of Gettysburg, Lincoln handed him command of the Army of the Potomac, a post he retained for the remainder of the Civil War. Although he led the Union to victory at Gettysburg, Meade was criticized for not pursuing Lee's retreating army.

Meade's short temper did not endear him to his men, and his dislike of reporters resulted in bad press. However, Meade remained a military man for the rest of his life, overseeing Reconstruction efforts in the South. Meade died of pneumonia in 1872.

THE WAR BETW

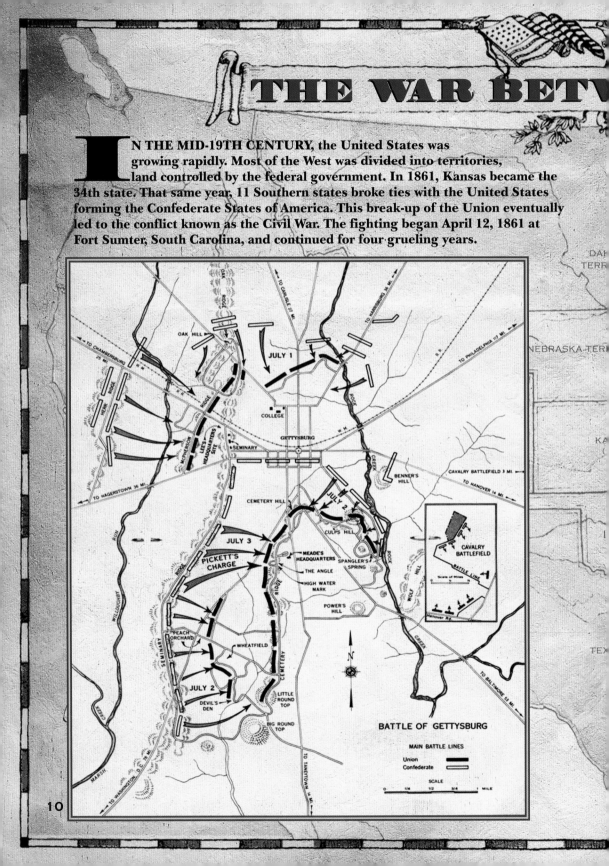

IN THE MID-19TH CENTURY, the United States was
growing rapidly. Most of the West was divided into territories,
land controlled by the federal government. In 1861, Kansas became the
34th state. That same year, 11 Southern states broke ties with the United States
forming the Confederate States of America. This break-up of the Union eventually
led to the conflict known as the Civil War. The fighting began April 12, 1861 at
Fort Sumter, South Carolina, and continued for four grueling years.

BATTLE OF GETTYSBURG

MAIN BATTLE LINES

Union
Confederate

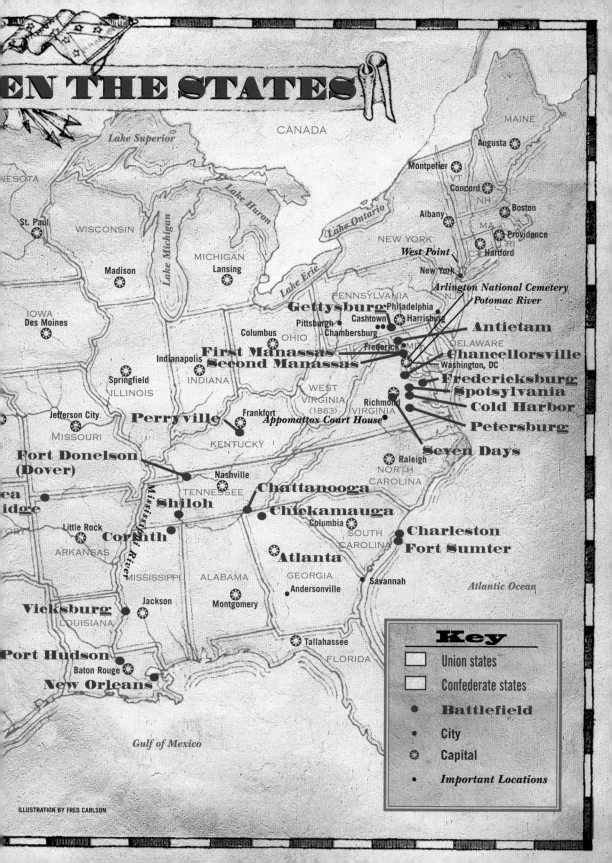

Lake Superior

CANADA

MAINE

Augusta ✪

Montpelier ✪

VT

Concord ✪

NH

Boston ✪

Albany ✪

MA

Providence ✪

St. Paul ✪

WISCONSIN

Lake Huron

Lake Michigan

MICHIGAN

Lansing ✪

Lake Ontario

NEW YORK

West Point

RI

✪ Hartford

CT

NESOTA

Madison ✪

Lake Erie

New York

IOWA

Des Moines ✪

Columbus

OHIO

PENNSYLVANIA

Arlington National Cemetery

Potomac River

Gettysburg

Philadelphia

Pittsburgh ●

Cashtown

Harrisburg ✪

NJ.

Indianapolis ✪

Chambersburg

Antietam

Frederick ●

MD

DELAWARE

First Manassas

Second Manassas

Washington, DC

Chancellorsville

Springfield ✪

ILLINOIS

INDIANA

WEST

VIRGINIA

(1863)

Richmond ✪

VIRGINIA

Fredericksburg

Spotsylvania

Cold Harbor

Jefferson City ✪

Perryville

Frankfort ✪

Appomattox Court House

Petersburg

MISSOURI

KENTUCKY

Seven Days

Fort Donelson

(Dover)

Nashville ✪

✪ Raleigh

NORTH

CAROLINA

ea

idge

TENNESSEE

Chattanooga

Shiloh

Chickamauga

Columbia

Little Rock ✪

Corinth

Columbus

SOUTH

CAROLINA

Charleston

Fort Sumter

ARKANSAS

Mississippi River

MISSISSIPPI

ALABAMA

Atlanta

GEORGIA

Andersonville ●

Savannah ●

Atlantic Ocean

Jackson ✪

Montgomery ✪

Vicksburg

LOUISIANA

Port Hudson

Baton Rouge ✪

✪ Tallahassee

FLORIDA

New Orleans

Gulf of Mexico

ILLUSTRATION BY FRED CARLSON

Key

☐ Union states

☐ Confederate states

● **Battlefield**

● City

✪ Capital

● *Important Locations*

Battle of Gettysburg: Facts and Figures

The Battle of Gettysburg was the largest of the Civil War battles, involving approximately 170,000 men, 70,000 horses, and 550 cannon. An estimated 7 million bullets were fired, and more soldiers died at Gettysburg than on any other battlefield of the Civil War.

General George G. Meade

Union
General George Gordon Meade
Commander, Army of the Potomac

Meade commanded 39 generals, including John Buford, John Fulton Reynolds, Abner Doubleday, Winfield Scott Hancock, George Armstrong Custer, Daniel Edgar Sickles, and Francis Channing Barlow.

Troops involved: **approximately 95,000**
Casualties (dead, wounded, and missing): **23,040**

Confederate
General Robert Edward Lee
Commander, Army of Northern Virginia

Lee commanded 30 generals, including James Longstreet, Ambrose Powell Hill, Richard Stoddert Ewell, Henry Heth, George Edward Pickett, James Ewell Brown "J.E.B." Stuart, Lewis Addison Armistead, Jubal Anderson Early, John Brown Gordon, and John Daniel Imboden.

Troops involved: **approximately 75,000**
Casualties (dead, wounded, and missing): **25,000 to 28,000**

General Robert E. Lee

Day One: July 1, 1863

At around 5:30 A.M., two divisions of Confederate soldiers, on a mission to obtain badly needed shoes and other supplies, met the vedettes and pickets that Union general John Buford had positioned just west of the village of Gettysburg. Almost immediately a battle broke out between divisions of the Southern and Northern armies. Fighting quickly escalated.

By 10:00 A.M., Confederate general Robert E. Lee had sent 25,000 soldiers into the fray. General George G. Meade responded with 20,000 Union soldiers (with more on the way), and soon both armies were heavily engaged. A Union gunner described the fighting: "For seven or eight minutes ensued probably the most desperate fight ever waged between artillery and infantry at close range without a particle of cover on either side… bullets hissing, humming and whistling everywhere; cannon roaring; smoke, dust, splinters, blood, wreck and carnage indescribable."

By midafternoon, Lee's army had pushed the Northerners back through Gettysburg to Cemetery Ridge on the southern edge of town. Late in the afternoon, the Union army established a strong line of defense from Culp's Hill, through Cemetery Ridge, and south to a hill called Little Round Top. They quickly prepared for a Confederate attack, but Lee's army did not advance. All the while, reinforcements for both sides converged on Gettysburg.

What had started as an accident had turned into a major engagement between Lee's Army of Northern Virginia and Meade's Army of the Potomac. At the end of the first day, it appeared that the South had the best chance of winning the Battle of Gettysburg.

It was the search for shoes and other basic supplies that brought Confederate soldiers into the town of Gettysburg, where Buford's men were watchful but unprepared for battle.

A Moment of Mercy

At around three o'clock on the afternoon of July 1, 1863, the Battle of Gettysburg came to an end for General Francis C. Barlow. Cut down by a Confederate rifle ball, the young Union officer sprawled helplessly on the field while the fighting blazed and roared around him. His troops were on the run, and the enemy was closing in. By all rights, Barlow should have been a dead man. But war and fate often pay little heed to what "should" be.

Moments before, Barlow had been in the thick of the struggle for control of a small knoll rising gently above the fields just north and slightly east of Gettysburg. This oval-shaped knob of land formed the "anchor" of the Union defenses above the town. A rippling line of Federal troops stretched from the knoll to the west before curving southward toward McPherson's Ridge. To Barlow's 1st Division fell the job of defending the right end of this line. On the flat plain below the ridge, the knoll was the only good spot to position his men and guns.

Gordon Is Impressed

Meanwhile, a Confederate brigade of 1,200 Georgia foot soldiers was advancing south toward the knoll. Their commander was General John B. Gordon, an experienced and respected officer. Riding a spirited black stallion, Gordon led his men to within 900 feet of Barlow's position. Then, their hair-raising yells splitting the air, the Georgians attacked. Already shaken by pounding Confederate cannon fire, Barlow's men bolted and ran.

As the men of the 1st Division fled across the fields, the victorious Gordon saw a sight that impressed him. "In the midst of the wild disorder in his ranks," he later wrote, "and through a storm of bullets, a Union officer was seeking to rally his men for a final stand."

That officer was General Barlow. Galloping down the knoll, the boyish-looking general tried valiantly to convince his troops to halt and reform their lines. As he did, a minié ball (cone-shaped rifle ball) struck him in the left side and passed completely through his body.

Enemies Meet

Barlow slid from his horse and collapsed in the grass. A frightening numbness spread through his arms and legs. Death, it seemed, was sure to follow. Then Barlow was dimly aware of someone kneeling beside him. Through pain-clouded eyes, Barlow looked up into the face of the enemy: Gordon, the very man who had led the attack on Barlow's knoll, was looking down on him.

Gordon kindly offered his fallen opponent a drink from his canteen. He learned Barlow's name and listened as the wounded man gasped out a last request. If Gordon survived the war, would he let Barlow's wife

Top: General Francis C. Barlow of Massachusetts was 28 years old at the Battle of Gettysburg. He had a reputation as a fierce fighter and strict leader. Bottom: A native of Georgia, John B. Gordon left his law practice to join the Confederate army in May 1861.

"Are you related to the Gordon who 'killed' me?" "I am the man, sir."

know that his last thoughts were of her and that he was willing to die for his country? Gordon was touched. Enemy or not, Barlow was clearly a devoted husband as well as a brave soldier. Stirred by these qualities, the Confederate general quickly summoned stretcher bearers and arranged to have Barlow carried to a shady place. Then he returned to his troops. Learning that Barlow's wife was with the Union army, Gordon later dispatched a courier to the Union camps to find her and escort her safely to her husband's side. Convinced that Barlow would be spending his last hours in loving hands, Gordon returned to the grim business of war. Months afterward, the name "General J.B. Gordon" appeared on the list of Confederate dead in a battle near Richmond. Thus, the two enemy generals who had met in a moment of mercy on the killing fields of Gettysburg were gone. They had both made the ultimate sacrifice for their causes. Or had they?

"To me, Barlow was dead," John Gordon related later. "To Barlow, I was dead. Nearly 15 years passed before either of us was undeceived."

A Surprise Return

Time went by. Then, at a banquet in Washington, D.C., in the late 1870s, a second-term U.S. senator was introduced to a prominent attorney. The senator's name was Gordon; the attorney's, Barlow.

"Are you related to the Barlow who was killed at Gettysburg?" asked the surprised senator.

"Why, I am the man, sir," replied the equally surprised attorney. "Are you related to the Gordon who 'killed' me?"

"I am the man, sir."

Explanations quickly followed. The minié ball that had pierced Barlow at Gettysburg had missed all his vital organs, and he had recovered. The Confederate general killed at Richmond was not this Gordon but a distant relative with the same first initials. Amazed and relieved, the two former generals took an immediate liking to each other. That affection deepened into an abiding friendship that lasted until Barlow's death in 1896.

Fast Fact

Barlow was the **only** Union general captured on July 1.

Day Two: July 2, 1863

July 2 dawned hot and sultry. General Robert E. Lee rose at 3:30 A.M. to plan the day's battle. Union general George G. Meade woke early to plan his strategy, too. He established a strong Union position on the south side of Gettysburg. General John Buford's cavalry was positioned near Little Round Top until it was ordered south to Maryland. Although General David McMurtrie Gregg's 2nd Division of Union cavalry was nearby, the absence of Buford's men meant that the left flank was temporarily unguarded.

Lee and his commanding officers decided that a large force of Confederates who had arrived during the night would attack the southern flank of the Union army while other Southern forces attacked the right flank. They hoped to strike the Union army with a surprisingly strong blow at a weak point.

Reportedly, one of Lee's officers, General James P. Longstreet, felt uneasy about the battle plan. He feared that the Union troops held too many strong positions on the battlefield. Thus, he slowly and reluctantly moved his troops into position. Precious time slipped away as the commanding officers readied for battle. Meanwhile, more Union soldiers arrived, and on the right flank they built walls of stone and logs for protection. Finally, at four that afternoon, the battle started. Time after time, the Confederates attacked the Union positions. But the Union lines held, and by nightfall the Confederate troops had lost many men and gained little ground.

As reinforcements arrived throughout the second day, officers readied their men for battles in several locations. The fighting broke out in the late afternoon and continued until dark.

Report of Colonel Joshua L. Chamberlain

Joshua L. Chamberlain commanded the 20th Maine Infantry. Before the war Chamberlain had been a college professor. His regiment played a key role in the Battle of Gettysburg, and his account helps us see how men (of both armies) had to work together to be effective.

Little Round Top, a rocky hilltop south of town, overlooks the battlefield. It was up to Chamberlain and his men to hold this strategic position for the Union.

After an hour or two of sleep by the roadside just before daybreak, we reached the heights southeasterly of Gettysburg about 7 A.M., July 2. Massed at first with the rest of the division…we were moved several times farther toward the left…, expecting every moment to be put into action and held strictly in line of battle….

Somewhere near 4 P.M. a sharp cannonade, at some distance to our left and front, was the signal for a sudden and rapid movement of our whole division in the direction of this firing, which grew

warmer as we approached. Passing an open field in the hollow ground in which some of our batteries were going into position, our brigade reached the skirt of a piece of woods, in the farther edge of which there was a heavy musketry fire, and when about to go forward into line we received…orders to move to the left at the double-quick, when we took a farm road crossing Plum Run in order to gain a rugged mountain spur called Granite Spur, or Little Round Top.

The enemy's artillery got range of our column as we were climbing the spur, and the crashing of the shells among the rocks and the tree tops made us move lively along the crest…. Passing to the southern slope of Little Round Top, Colonel Vincent indicated to me the ground my regiment was to occupy, informing me that this was the extreme left of our general line, and that a desperate attack was expected in order to turn that position, concluding by telling me I was to "hold that ground at all hazards." That was the last word I heard from him.

Holding Little Round Top

In order to commence by making my right firm, I formed my regiment on the right into line, giving such direction to the line as should best secure the advantage of the rough, rocky, and stragglingly wooded ground.

When his commanding officer was killed on Little Round Top, Joshua Chamberlain made the risky decision to order a bayonet charge down the hill to halt the Confederate advance.

The line faced generally toward a more conspicuous eminence southwest of ours, which is known as Sugar Loaf, or [Great] Round Top. Between this and my position intervened a smooth and thinly wooded hollow. My line formed, I immediately detached Company B, Captain [Walter G.] Morrill commanding, to extend from my left flank across this hollow as a line of skirmishers, with directions to act as occasion might dictate, to prevent a surprise on my exposed flank and rear.

The artillery fire on our position had meanwhile been constant and heavy, but my formation was scarcely complete when the artillery was replaced by a vigorous infantry assault upon the center of our brigade to my right, but it very soon involved the right of my regiment and gradually extended along my entire front. The action was quite sharp and at close quarters.

In the midst of this, an officer from my center informed me that some important movement of the enemy was going on in his front, beyond that of the line with which we were engaged. Mounting a large rock, I was able to see a considerable body of the enemy moving by the flank in rear of their line engaged, and passing from the direction of the foot of Great Round Top through the valley toward the front of my left. The close engagement not allowing any change of front, I immediately stretched my regiment to the left, so that it was nearly at right angles with my right, thus occupying about twice the extent of our ordinary front. My officers and men understood my wishes so well that this movement was executed under fire, the right wing keeping up fire, without giving the enemy any occasion to seize or even to suspect their advantage. But we were not a moment too soon; the enemy's flanking column having gained their desired direction, burst upon my left, where they evidently had expected an unguarded flank, with great demonstration. We opened a brisk fire at close range, which was so sudden and effective that they soon fell back among the rocks and low trees in the valley, only to burst forth again with a shout, and rapidly advanced, firing as they came. They pushed up to within a dozen yards of us before the terrible effectiveness of our fire compelled them to break and take shelter.

"We opened a brisk fire at close range, which was so sudden and effective that they soon fell back among the rocks and low trees in the valley, only to burst forth again with a shout."

Fighting Hand to Hand

They renewed the assault on our whole front, and for an hour the fighting was severe. Squads of the enemy broke through our line in several places, and the fight was literally hand to hand. The edge of the fight rolled backward and forward like a wave. The dead and wounded were now in our front and then in our rear. Forced from our position, we desperately recovered it, and pushed the enemy down to the foot of the slope. The intervals of the struggle were seized to remove the wounded (and those of the enemy also), to gather ammunition from the cartridge boxes of disabled friend

or foe on the field, and even to secure better muskets than the Enfields, which we found did not stand service well. Rude shelters were thrown up of the loose rocks that covered the ground.

Captain [Orpheus S.] Woodward, commanding the 83rd Pennsylvania Volunteers, on my right, gallantly maintaining his fight, judiciously and with hearty cooperation made his movements conform to my necessities, so that my right was at no time exposed to a flank attack.

The enemy seemed to have gathered all their energies for their final assault. We had gotten our thin line into as good a shape as possible, when a strong force emerged from the scrub wood in the valley [to the left], as well as I could judge, in two lines in echelon by the right, and opening a heavy fire, the first line came on us as [if] they meant to sweep everything before them. We opened on them as well as we could with our scanty ammunition snatched from the field.

A wooded area below Little Round Top hid the enemy, giving Chamberlain's men less time to react to an attack. The Confederate soldiers took full advantage of this and fought aggressively.

The bayonet charge, shown here, is one of warfare's most brutal fights. With a bayonet attached, the rifle becomes a sharp and deadly blade.

It did not seem possible to withstand another shock like this now coming on. Our loss had been severe. One-half of my left wing had fallen, and a third of my regiment lay just behind us, dead or badly wounded. At this moment my anxiety was increased by a great roar of musketry in my rear, on the farther or northerly slope of Little Round Top. The bullets from this attack struck into my left rear, and I feared that the enemy might have nearly surrounded the Little Round Top, and only a desperate chance was left for us. My ammunition was soon exhausted. My men were firing their last shot and getting ready to "club" their muskets.

Fix Bayonets!

It was imperative to strike before we were struck by this overwhelming force in a hand-to-hand fight, which we could not probably have withstood or survived. At that crisis, I ordered the bayonet. The word was enough. It ran like fire along the line, from man to man, and rose into a shout, with which they sprang forward upon the enemy, now not 30 yards away. The effect was surprising; many of the enemy's first line threw down their arms and surrendered. An officer fired his pistol at my head with one hand, while he handed me his sword with the other. Holding fast by our right, and swinging forward our left, we made an extended "right wheel," before which the enemy's second line broke and fell back, fighting from tree to tree, many being captured, until we had swept the valley and cleared the front of nearly our entire brigade.

Meantime Captain Morrill with his skirmishers (sent out from my left flank), with some dozen or fifteen of the U.S. Sharpshooters who had put themselves under his direction, fell upon the enemy as they were breaking, and by his demonstrations, as well as his well-directed fire, added much to the effect of the charge.

Having thus cleared the valley, and driven the enemy up the western slope of the Great Round Top, not wishing to press so far out as to hazard the ground I was to hold by leaving it exposed to a sudden rush of the enemy, I succeeded (although with some effort to stop my men, who declared they were "on the road to Richmond") in getting the regiment into good order and resuming our original position.

> "My ammunition was soon exhausted. My men were firing their last shot and getting ready to 'club' their muskets."

Assessing the Losses

Four hundred prisoners, including two field and several line officers, were sent to the rear. These were mainly from the 15th and 47th Alabama Regiments, with some of the Fourth and Fifth Texas. One hundred and fifty of the enemy were found killed and wounded.... We went into the fight with 386, all told — 358 guns. Every pioneer and musician who could carry a musket went into the ranks. Even the sick and foot-sore, who could not keep up in the march, came up as soon as they could find their regiments, and took their places in line of battle.... Some prisoners I had under guard, under sentence of court-martial, I was obliged to put into the fight, and they bore their part well, for which I shall recommend a commutation of their sentence.

The loss, so far as I can ascertain it, is 136 — 30 of whom were killed, and among the wounded are many mortally.

Day Three: July 3, 1863

The next day General Robert E. Lee tried once again to destroy the Union army. Confederate cannon fired on the enemy, but the Union soldiers lay low behind rocks and rails. Consequently, the Confederate cannon fire caused few injuries. Then the Union troops opened up with their own cannon. For more than an hour, the cannon blasted away at each other. Union officers watching the battle finally decided to stop firing their cannon and save ammunition.

The Confederate officers concluded that their cannon had destroyed several Union strongholds. Therefore, the officers ordered 12,000 of their soldiers to attack the middle of Meade's defensive line. As the Confederate army moved forward, Union soldiers opened up with cannon fire and guns. Confederate soldiers fell by the thousands. Only a few hundred reached the ridge, where many fell to Union bayonets. Others were taken prisoner.

The offensive had failed. About 3,000 Confederate soldiers lay dead as a result of three days of hard fighting. Many more would die from wounds or disease. Devastated by the defeat, Lee and his troops retreated south.

Historians call Gettysburg the high-water mark of the Civil War because the South would never again strongly advance so far into the North. Lee had lost thousands of fighting men, and his troops had consumed many badly needed supplies. The South had lost its momentum and all hope of obtaining European support. Two years later, Lee surrendered his army to General Ulysses S. Grant at Appomattox Court House, Virginia, but in many people's minds, the war had been lost at Gettysburg.

The final day of fighting culminated in General Pickett's ill-fated Confederate charge across open ground in an attempt to break the Union line on Cemetery Ridge.

Pickett's Charge

Confederate soldiers who survived the advance under heavy cannon fire encountered Union bayonets on Cemetery Ridge.

A solemn silence stretched uneasily between the Union and Confederate troops that morning of July 3, 1863, following the early-morning battle over Culp's Hill at the far right of the Union line. The stillness was broken by the cries of the wounded and the groans of dying horses, but the artillery was quiet — for the moment. The bloody and bitter Battle of Gettysburg had been raging for two days, and this, the third and final day, would decide the outcome of the greatest battle of the Civil War and, ultimately, of the war itself.

Confederate Momentum

The Union troops were worried. Confederate forces had attacked nearly every segment of their line, and victory seemed just out of the Confederates' reach. The Confederate army, properly known as the Army of Northern Virginia, had thrashed the North soundly many times, most recently at Chancellorsville, Virginia, only two months before. It seemed as though nothing could get in the Confederates' way.

General George G. Meade had held a meeting with his generals the night before. They had voted to "stay and fight it out," defending Gettysburg as Union domain, but not to lead any attacks against the Southern forces. They would let the Confederates take the offensive if they wanted, but the Federals would remain in their trenches and behind the stone walls of Cemetery Ridge.

General James Longstreet, (left) who opposed Lee's plan, reluctantly relayed the order to General George Pickett, whose men were fresh and ready for battle.

A Big Gamble

General Robert E. Lee, waiting with his army across the fields, had two options: Either the Army of Northern Virginia could make a final, spectacular attack to try to break the Union line, or they could admit defeat and retreat back to their home territory. Lee and his troops were unwilling to give up so easily. They knew that if they won this battle, they could march farther into the North, or perhaps capture Washington, D.C., more than 70 miles away. If they held Washington, they could very well win the war.

It was a big gamble, and the stakes were high, but in the end Lee decided that taking the offensive was worth the risk.

The day before, the Confederates had made repeated attacks on the Union flanks (sides). Today, Lee planned to make a full-scale assault on the center of the Union line, scattering and destroying the Army of the Potomac once and for all.

Generals Pickett and Longstreet

Of course, the disadvantages of the plan had to be weighed. Only one fresh division of Southerners was available. General George G. Pickett's all-Virginia infantry, guarding supply wagons for the first two days of battle, had seen no action at Gettysburg. Despite the loss of thousands of men, Pickett's infantry was itching to fight. Pickett, with his drooping mustache and long, curled hair, looked like a swashbuckling cavalier, and he, too, was eager to see battle and perhaps win everlasting glory at Gettysburg.

Another problem was that General James P. Longstreet, the corps commander, opposed the plan altogether and tried unsuccessfully to convince Lee to launch an attack on the Union's left flank instead.

Finally, the attacking Confederates had to cross a nearly mile-long stretch of open ground before they could confront the enemy. The Federals had dug in infantry equipped with long-range rifles to defend their position on Cemetery Ridge, and they were backed by cannon besides. The strategy of pitting massed troops against weapons designed to slaughter large numbers of soldiers could spell wholesale destruction for the South.

Underestimating the Union

But Lee's plan seemed solid enough. A fierce barrage of cannon fire would weaken the Union forces. This would be followed by Pickett's three brigades spearheading the assault on the Union center. To tie up the loose ends, General Richard S. Ewell would go after the Federals' right flank, and General J.E.B. Stuart's famous cavalry would circle around to the rear, ready to surprise the enemy when they retreated.

Lee, it seemed, had thought of everything. But for all his wisdom, he had underestimated the enemy. The Federals, used to marching deep into enemy territory amid the resentment of the Southern populace, had often been defeated by the heroic and often outnumbered Confederates. Now the tables were turned. The Federals in Pennsylvania found themselves local heroes and this time were defending their homeland against the Southern invaders.

Fast Fact

In their favor, the Union cavalry carried repeating rifles that could fire up to

20

rounds per minute, compared with the Confederates' firearms, which shot only

4.

The Saddest Day

A little after one o'clock that afternoon, the blast and roar of cannon fire interrupted the hazy stillness. The thundering of nearly 300 cannon could be heard far and wide.

Meanwhile, nearly 12,000 Confederate soldiers had been forming their lines all along Seminary Ridge under the cover of ridges and woods. At three o'clock, Longstreet reluctantly gave the order for the charge to advance. "I could see the desperate and hopeless nature of the charge and the hopeless slaughter it would cause," he wrote long after. "That day at Gettysburg was one of the saddest of my life."

Nearly 300 cannon blasted relentlessly for hours on the afternoon of July 3. Pickett lost more than half his men in the daring offensive.

With parade-ground precision, the Confederates marched valiantly forth — Pickett's men on the right, General James J. Pettigrew's soldiers on the left — supported by even more troops in the rear. A mass of gray infantry flowed unfalteringly toward the Union line in a solid wave nearly a mile wide. The Federals had never seen such a sight. They waited silently, withholding fire until the Confederates were a little closer.

When the order to fire was given, it did not take the Federals long to act. They fired, and gray-clad soldiers fell in clumps. The survivors surged forward, faster now. The famous "rebel yell" rang out as the men in gray closed the gap between themselves and the Union line. At first it seemed as though the torrent of men could not be stopped, but as they continued to fall, a Union victory seemed closer at hand. The few Confederates who made it behind the Union lines had little chance of survival. Many surrendered, and those who did not fought valiantly to the end.

Meanwhile, J.E.B. Stuart's cavalry was repulsed at the rear of the battlefield by Union troops, including General George A. Custer's horsemen. When Stuart's men saw that the battle was lost, they turned back to Seminary Ridge.

The Rebel Army Retreats

General Lee rode into the fields to praise and rally the survivors of Pickett's Charge. "It's all my fault," he told his men sadly. "It is I who have lost this fight, and you must help me out of it the best way you can." He believed that Meade would order a counterattack to take advantage of the disorganized state of Lee's army and perhaps destroy the Army of Northern Virginia once and for all. But the expected counterattack never came. Meade neglected to follow through on his victory. Instead, he gave the enemy time to regroup and allowed them to withdraw to Virginia the following day under cover of a heavy rainstorm. Meade has been criticized for that error ever since.

Both the Union and the Confederate forces suffered enormous losses that day at Gettysburg. Of the nearly 12,000 Confederate soldiers who took part in Pickett's Charge, perhaps only half returned to fight again.

Historians say that Pickett's Charge is representative of the entire Confederate war effort. Just as the men in Pickett's Charge carried a sense of unbeatability onto the fields around Gettysburg, the entire South believed it was indestructible. In both cases, a deep sense of matchless valor met with disaster.

Key Players

George E. Pickett
1825–1875

From the time he graduated from West Point military academy in 1825, George Pickett was a career soldier. Before the Civil War, he was an officer in the U.S.–Mexican War and served in the Washington Territory.

When Virginia seceded from the United States, Richmond-born Pickett resigned from the U.S. Army to join the Confederate cause. In October 1861, Pickett commanded a division at Fredericksburg, where the Union dealt him a heavy blow.

He may be best known for the courageous but fateful charge he led at Gettysburg on July 3, 1863. Pickett's Charge has gone down in history as a deciding factor in the South's ultimate defeat.

News From the Battlefield

C.C. Coffin and Samuel Wilkeson were among the more than 300 reporters who followed the Union armies from battle to battle during the Civil War. They provided on-the-spot accounts of major battles, and their information was often the first report the War Department and President Abraham Lincoln had of how a battle was progressing.

Two Ace Reporters

Coffin was not just an ace reporter; he was a gifted musician as well. His knowledge of notes and tones helped him distinguish what ammunition was whizzing around his head. Known as being brave and steadfast under fire, this well-educated New Hampshire native was one of the few news correspondents to stay on the job throughout the war. His reports of the Battle of Gettysburg appeared in the *Boston Journal*.

Also reporting from Gettysburg was Wilkeson. Wilkeson had been involved in journalism since his grammar school days, when he had published a weekly newspaper. Later trained as a lawyer, Wilkeson left his legal practice to pursue a newspaper career. At the beginning of the war, he was the *New York Tribune*'s Washington correspondent.

Aside from reporting the details of each battle, reporters such as Coffin and Wilkeson compiled lists of the dead and wounded, interviewed prisoners of war, and sketched pictures of the people and events they saw. During the terror and confusion of battle, they took care of the wounded and offered whatever other assistance they could provide. Reporting was a hazardous job, for sickness and injury struck those observing the battle as well as those fighting it.

C.C. Coffin of New Hampshire covered the war for the *Boston Journal*. Besides writing reports, Coffin tended wounded soldiers and helped out with administrative tasks.

A Newspaper Boom

The Civil War had created a boom in news publishing and had changed the appearance and nature of newspapers. The pace of news reporting quickened as people demanded the latest accounts of fast-breaking events. Americans were emotionally, physically, and financially caught up in this great conflict, and they wanted to know the latest news from the front. After a great battle, a newspaper's circulation often increased to five times its normal level. The war inspired the creation of Sunday papers, and several daily editions were common. These afternoon and evening editions were called "extras" because initially they were extra editions put out after significant events.

With horse-drawn carts for easy mobility, newspaper vendors set up shop near battlefields and offered a choice of papers.

The armies also provided a huge market for newspaper sales. Pickets, the front-line sentinels, commonly swapped newspapers, along with tobacco and other prized items, with their enemy counterparts.

During the war, news publishing also became more profitable, and technical innovations came into widespread use. Expensive telegraphed reports mushroomed from two to three columns per paper to two to three pages. Improvements in typesetting and printing also were made, and headline sizes were increased greatly to produce a dramatic effect. As bylines became widely used, formerly anonymous reporters became celebrities.

Witnessing the Battle

Both Wilkeson and Coffin arrived at Gettysburg on July 3, 1863, the third day of the battle. They witnessed the Confederate bombardment and Pickett's Charge, which marked the climax of the Battle of Gettysburg.

On that day, the armies had gathered on two roughly parallel ridges — the Confederates on Seminary Ridge and the Federals on Cemetery Ridge. At about 1 P.M., General Robert E. Lee's artillery on Seminary Ridge opened fire. "Every size and form of shell known to British and American gunnery shrieked, whirled, moaned, and whistled and wrathfully fluttered over our ground," Wilkeson wrote. "Not an orderly — not an ambulance — not a straggler was to be seen upon the plain swept by this tempest of orchestral death thirty minutes after it commenced."

The Federal guns returned the fire, but shortly after 3 P.M., either as a ruse or to preserve ammunition, they were slowly silenced. At the pause of gunfire, about 12,000 Confederate soldiers moved across the mile-long valley separating the two ridges. They marched at a walk — one hundred yards a minute. Blasted by the Union artillery, they continued on.

Describing the horrendous hand-to-hand combat that ensued, Coffin wrote, "Men fire into each other's faces, not five feet apart. There are bayonet thrusts, sabre-strokes, pistol shots; cool, deliberate movements on the part of some, — hot, passionate, desperate efforts with others,... There are ghastly heaps of dead men."

When the battle was over, victory belonged to the Union, but both armies had suffered devastating losses. Wilkeson sat beside the body of his 19-year-old son while he wrote his account of Gettysburg. Lieutenant Bayard Wilkeson had been injured on the first day of the battle and had died from lack of medical attention to his wounds.

Coffin galloped away in search of telegraph wires to relay his story. Most had been cut, so he boarded a hospital train and made his way back to Boston. Once there, he locked himself in a room, wrote his copy, then threw himself down on a stack of newspapers and slept for 24 hours.

Pictures of Gettysburg

When the battle ended, artists and photographers descended on Gettysburg. Alexander Gardner rumbled into town with two horse-drawn darkrooms and began recording the scene. By the time photographer Mathew Brady arrived, the dead had been buried, so he documented the landscape, taking panoramic shots of Little Round Top and Cemetery Hill. In 1866, after the Civil War had concluded, artist Peter Frederick Rothermel tramped the fields with former soldiers. He sketched faces and locations, then created a series of paintings immortalizing the battlefield.

Tending the Wounded

No one knows exactly how many men lay dead or wounded between Cemetery Ridge and Seminary Ridge after the Battle of Gettysburg, but almost 50,000 is an educated guess. About 7,000 of those died on the battlefield, and perhaps another 3,000 succumbed later to their wounds.

On July 4, at four in the afternoon, what was left of the Confederate army began to retreat south. Forty percent of General Robert E. Lee's army — about 28,000 men — were casualties. Any man who could hobble had to march. Even so, the immobile were so numerous that the caravan of ambulances and wagons carrying the wounded stretched for 17 miles.

General Lee assigned General John Imboden the "arduous, responsible, and dangerous" duty of escorting the ambulance train, "that vast procession of misery," to Virginia. Rain poured down in

After the fighting ended, the armies of the North and South moved out of Gettysburg, leaving thousands of dead and wounded soldiers. The caravan of Confederate ambulances bound for Virginia stretched 17 miles.

Civil War Nurses

When President Abraham Lincoln called up 75,000 volunteers for the Union army in April 1861, no organized medical corps, army nurse corps, or field hospital service existed. At first the nursing gap was filled by women in religious orders. But there were not nearly enough nursing sisters to go around, and they were soon joined by lay women and men who had no nursing training at all.

Two months after the start of the war, Dorothea Dix was appointed superintendent of the female nurses of the army. Dix recruited 2,000 women, each of whom had to be at least 30 years old. The chief duties of these women were dressing wounds, administering medicine, and overseeing the preparation of food.

The Confederate army did not appoint a nursing director but did give some authority to Sally Tompkins, who set up a successful hospital in a private home.

The U.S. Sanitary Commission, the Christian Commission, and the American Association for the Relief of Misery on the Battlefield helped with battleground nursing and hygiene.

torrents all day and all night, and some of the men had no food for 36 hours. The jolting ride in the wagons, all without springs and many without even a bed of straw, caused the men so much pain that some begged to get out. But Imboden was under strict orders from Lee not to stop under any circumstances because Lee feared pursuit by the Union army.

Imboden later said that that day and night taught him more about the horrors of war than all his other experiences put together.

Somehow most of the wounded men survived the 24-hour trip to Williamsport, on the Maryland–West Virginia border. There the wagons halted, and surgeons could finally attend to the soldiers.

Imboden had planned to cross the Potomac River at Williamsport, but the bridge had been destroyed and the river was too high to be forded. The wounded had to wait several days, while the river fell and a pontoon bridge was built, until they could cross.

Left Behind

Many injured Confederate soldiers could not be moved and had to be left at Gettysburg to be picked up with the Union men. Many doctors and medical attendants had marched away with the Army of the Potomac, and the remaining surgeons were hard pressed to care for their own 14,000 wounded soldiers, let alone the captured Confederates. The townspeople of Gettysburg threw themselves into the task, but even so, there were 10 wounded soldiers for every man, woman, and child in the village.

Some families of the fallen soldiers came to Gettysburg as soon as they heard the news about their boys. They arrived carrying baskets of bread, vegetables, applesauce, and jelly. They brought home remedies such as spirits of camphor and turpentine and talcum powder. The women made bandages by scraping cotton cloth with a knife, then using the soft fuzz to dress wounds.

> "There are no words in the English language to express the sufferings I witnessed today."
> — a Quaker nurse

Volunteers to the Rescue

Aside from family members, many other patriotic citizens volunteered to help the wounded. Doctors and nurses traveled from nearby cities to Gettysburg, and groups of churchwomen and Ladies Aid members put in long, exhausting hours. Many people who sent packages of food and supplies addressed them simply "Gettysburg."

Women walked through the battle hospitals at night, comforting the soldiers, wiping their faces with cool cloths, offering them cups of tea and soup, and writing letters home. They laid straw in the hospital tents and piled up boxes to keep the wind from blowing through the flimsy shelters. They prepared *panada*, an invalid food made by mixing rusks (dry bread) with melted butter, sugar, and brandy, then pouring boiling water over the mixture.

Stretcher bearers were still gathering up the fallen several days after the final battle. Many men had to lie in the muddy fields, exposed to sun and rain, until they could be loaded onto hay wagons and carried to public buildings and farmhouses to be cared for. Soldiers lay stretched out on church pews that had been pushed together to make beds. A red banner flew over every building that

Fast Fact

Of all the Civil War battles, Gettysburg had the most — more than

50,000

— casualties.

Doctors, nurses, family members, and townspeople spent weeks dealing with the devastating aftermath of the battle. Surgeons set up makeshift hospitals in nearby farmhouses and helped as many wounded soldiers as possible.

sheltered the wounded. A Quaker nurse said, "There are no words in the English language to express the sufferings I witnessed today."

Special trains took the men to Baltimore, Philadelphia, and Harrisburg to be treated in better-equipped and better-staffed hospitals. By early August, one month after the end of the battle, 16,000 men had been moved. The most serious cases were still being cared for just outside Gettysburg at Camp Letterman, a central hospital of tents that had been established at the end of July. When the national cemetery was dedicated on November 19, a handful of the last of these wounded had places of honor in the group marching to the dedication stand.

Burying the dead was a painful task. Men dug trenches seven feet wide and two feet deep, then buried the bodies in long rows of 50 to 100. When known, names and regiments were written on wooden headboards. Later, the bodies of Union soldiers were grouped by state and reburied on Cemetery Hill in the national cemetery. It was not until the early 1870s that the bodies of the Confederate dead were moved to Southern cemeteries.

Legends of General Lee

On many starry nights during the Civil War, Northern and Southern troops alike gathered around their campfires for an evening of storytelling. Sharing tales of bravery and heroic feats helped the soldiers keep up their morale, and talking openly about their fears and the horrors they had seen seemed to ease their burdens. Some of the tales they told began to circulate, passed among troops by word of mouth, sent home in letters, or published in small-town newspapers. After the war was over, favorite stories continued to be retold at family gatherings and meetings of veterans' organizations. Although their historical accuracy is no longer known, many charming stories have been preserved as part of the legacy we call "folk history."

Folk stories of the Civil War seem to share certain common characteristics. Ordinary people often became the heroes of these tales, and the good or bad qualities of public figures such as President Abraham Lincoln often were exaggerated until the people resembled the characters of ancient mythology. The following are three tales from Gettysburg that focus on General Robert E. Lee. They all show that he was respected by Northerners and Southerners alike.

Despite their differences, Northerners and Southerners considered General Robert E. Lee an honorable man and a brilliant leader.

The Salute

Under the scorching June sun, General Robert E. Lee led his Confederate troops northward. As the tired soldiers marched across the fields of Pennsylvania, a young Pennsylvania Dutch girl came running out of a farmhouse, fiercely waving a Union flag. Calling his troops to a halt, Lee studied the face of the girl standing defiantly before him. Then he raised his arm and ceremoniously saluted her before resuming his march.

Later, as the troops were setting up camp for the night, the Southern general overheard a conversation between two soldiers who were criticizing him for his salute to the enemy flag. Lee corrected them, saying, "I saluted not the enemy, but the bravery of a young patriot and the flag of a great nation that I once served."

The Wounded Union Soldier

It was clearly a victory for the Union forces, and General Robert E. Lee had no choice but to call retreat. As he led his defeated Confederate soldiers from the Gettysburg battlefield on that fateful day in 1863, a wounded Union soldier taunted him with a cry of "Hurrah for the Union!" To the astonishment of the young private, Lee swung his horse around and dismounted. Kneeling in the dirt beside the boy, the defeated general lightly touched his fingertips to the bloody wound that had caused the soldier to fall. "My son," he said gently, "I hope you will soon be well."

As Lee rode away, the wounded soldier burst into tears, both because of this unexpected act of kindness and because he feared he would die there. The soldier did not die, but recovered to tell his story.

The Favor

It was June 28, just days before the Battle of Gettysburg would take place, and Ellen McLellan sighed as she peered into her larder. There was no meat left, and she had used the last of her flour the day before, so she could not even bake bread to feed her hungry children. Several days earlier, Confederate troops had moved into McLellan's hometown of Chambersburg, Pennsylvania, seizing control of the stores and mills and leaving few provisions for the townspeople.

With a plan in mind, McLellan set out for the Confederate camp. She was afraid of the soldiers but had heard they were Southern gentlemen who would not harm a lady. On the outskirts of town, she asked a soldier for directions to General Robert E. Lee's tent. Standing before him, she said, "Sir, as you have taken control of our mill, I have come on behalf of the citizens of Chambersburg to beg just a little flour for the purpose of baking bread."

After asking her name, the general replied, "I shall see that the mill is opened to the townspeople, Mrs. McLellan. Is there anything else?"

"Yes, sir. I would like to request your autograph."

General Lee was astonished. "Madam, do you realize that I am your enemy, and that having my signature in your possession would be very inappropriate?"

Despite the general's warning, McLellan left Lee's tent with his autograph, as well as his word to provide the townspeople with flour. Unfortunately, the fighting at Gettysburg broke out before he could keep his promise.

Fast Fact

Nearly
170,000
soldiers fought at Gettysburg, a town of
2,400
people.

'A Few Appropriate Remarks'

While Union and Confederate forces battled ferociously at Gettysburg, the Union's Commander in Chief, Abraham Lincoln, waited in Washington for news from the front.

Hour after hour during those anxious days and nights, an eyewitness remembered, Lincoln's tall form could be found at the War Department, bent over stacks of telegrams from the battle. On the third day, his burden grew even heavier: His fragile wife, Mary, was thrown from her carriage in a freak accident and suffered a head injury.

Lincoln addressed a crowd of about 15,000 men, women, and children. Few would have predicted that the speech was destined to be one of the most famous in American history.

News of Victory

Finally, after 72 hours of unrelieved tension, Lincoln learned that the North had prevailed at Gettysburg. Privately, he was disappointed that his generals did not follow up their victory by pursuing the Confederates as they fled south. Publicly, he sent the army the "highest honors" for their "great success." He seemed to sense that, flawed or not, the Battle of Gettysburg would be a turning point in the Civil War.

The citizens of Pennsylvania, also aware of their new place in history, moved quickly to create a national cemetery for the thousands of casualties at Gettysburg. A dedication ceremony was planned, and Lincoln received an invitation to attend. He was not, however, asked to deliver the major speech of the day. That honor was given to a New England statesman and professional orator named Edward Everett. Lincoln, one organizer worried, was incapable of speaking "upon such a great and solemn occasion." The president was asked merely to give "a few appropriate remarks." Yet aware that the event was momentous, Lincoln accepted the halfhearted invitation.

As the day grew near, Lincoln's wife urged him to reconsider. Their young son, Tad, had fallen ill, and Mary Lincoln was near hysteria. (Only a year earlier, their middle child, Willie, had died.) On the morning of his father's departure, Tad was so sick he could not eat breakfast. Lincoln himself felt unwell, but he decided to go anyway. With little fanfare, he boarded a train for the slow journey to Gettysburg.

The legend that the president waited until he was on the train to prepare his speech and then scribbled it on the back of an envelope is untrue. Lincoln carefully wrote at least one version of his speech on White House stationery before he left and probably rewrote it in his bedroom in Gettysburg the night before delivering it.

On Thursday, November 19, a balmy, Indian summer day, the six-foot-four Lincoln mounted an undersized horse and joined a mournful procession through the town and toward the new cemetery near the battlefield. An immense throng had gathered there, and as Lincoln arrived at the speakers' platform, every man in the crowd respectfully removed his hat. The president was greeted with "a perfect silence."

Lincoln's brief speech at Gettysburg honored the sacrifice made by the soldiers who died there, and challenged the audience to rededicate themselves to the cause of freedom.

'Is That All?'

For two hours, Everett held the spectators spellbound with his rich voice and soaring words. A hymn followed; then Lincoln rose to

Thousands of graves encircle the Soldiers' National Monument (background) at Gettysburg National Military Park. The cemetery, designed by landscape architect William Saunders, was completed in 1872.

speak. "Four score and seven years ago," Lincoln began in a high-pitched voice. He spoke for barely three minutes, ending with the words "government of the people, by the people, for the people, shall not perish from the earth."

Almost as soon as he had begun, he sat down. Some eyewitnesses recalled a smattering of applause, but others heard "not a word, not a cheer, not a shout." A stenographer leaned over to Lincoln and asked, "Is that all?" Embarrassed, Lincoln replied, "Yes — for the present." A photographer in the crowd, fussing with his camera, had not even had time to take a picture.

Lincoln thought his speech was a failure. "People are disappointed," he grimly told the man who had introduced him. To add to his misery, he came down with a mild case of smallpox on the trip back to Washington.

'Not Entirely a Failure'

Many who listened to the speech felt differently, however. While some newspapers dismissed the speech as "silly," "dull," and "commonplace," another correctly predicted that the Gettysburg Address would "live among the annals of man." Perhaps the best compliment of all came from Everett. A few days after they both had spoken at Gettysburg, he wrote to Lincoln, saying he wished he had come "as close to the central idea of the occasion, in two hours, as you did in two minutes." Lincoln replied, telling Everett how pleased he was that "the little I did say was not entirely a failure."

Today, Abraham Lincoln's Gettysburg Address is remembered as one of the great speeches of all time.

The Gettysburg Address

Four score and seven years ago our fathers brought forth, upon this continent, a new nation, conceived in liberty, and dedicated to the proposition that all men are created equal.

Now we are engaged in a great civil war, testing whether that nation, or any nation so conceived, and so dedicated, can long endure. We are met here on a great battlefield of the war. We have come to dedicate a portion of it as a final resting place for those who here gave their lives that the nation might live. It is altogether fitting and proper that we should do this.

But in a larger sense we can not dedicate — we can not consecrate — we can not hallow this ground. The brave men, living and dead, who struggled here, have consecrated it far above our poor power to add or detract. The world will little note, nor long remember, what we say here, but can never forget what they did here. It is for us the living, rather to be dedicated here to the unfinished work which they have, thus far, so nobly carried on. It is rather for us to be here dedicated to the great task remaining before us — that from these honored dead we take increased devotion to that cause for which they here gave the last full measure of devotion — that we here highly resolve that these dead shall not have died in vain; that this nation shall have a new birth of freedom; and that this government of the people, by the people, for the people shall not perish from the earth.

Fast Fact

Lincoln's speech was

268

words long. Everett's was more than

13,600.

CIVIL WAR

1860

NOV 6
Abraham Lincoln is elected 16th president of the United States.

Lincoln

1861

FEB 9
Formation of the Confederate States of America (CSA) by secessionist states South Carolina, Mississippi, Florida, Alabama, Georgia, Louisiana, and Texas. Jefferson Davis elected CSA president.

MAR 4
Lincoln's inauguration

APR 12

Fort Sumter (South Carolina) Civil War begins with Confederate attack under Gen. Pierre Beauregard.

APR 15
Lincoln issues proclamation calling

for 75,000 troops. Gen. Winfield Scott becomes commander of Union army.

APR 17
Virginia joins CSA, followed by Arkansas, Tennessee, and North Carolina.

APR 20
Gen. Robert E. Lee resigns from U.S. Army and accepts command in Confederate army.

Davis

JUL 21
First Manassas (Virginia) Gen. Thomas J. "Stonewall" Jackson defeats Gen. Irvin McDowell.

NOV 1
Gen. George B. McClellan assumes command of Union forces.

1862

FEB 11-16
Fort Donelson (Tennessee) Gen. Ulysses S. Grant breaks major Confederate stronghold.

MAR
McClellan begins Peninsular Campaign, heading to Richmond,

Virginia, the Confederate capital.

APR 6-7
Shiloh (Tennessee) Grant defeats Beauregard and Gen. A.S. Johnston. Heavy losses on both sides.

APR 24

New Orleans (Louisiana) Gen. David Farragut leads 17 Union gunboats up Mississippi River and takes New Orleans, the South's most important seaport.

JUN 25- JUL 1
Seven Days (Virginia) Six major battles are fought over seven days near Richmond, Virginia. Lee is victorious, protecting the Confederate capital from Union occupation.

Halleck

JUL 18
Lincoln turns over command to Gen. Henry W. Halleck.

AUG 29-30
Second Manassas (Virginia) Jackson and Gen. James Longstreet defeat Gen. John Pope.

SEP 17
Antietam (Maryland) McClellan narrowly defeats Lee. Bloodiest day in American military history: 23,000 casualties.

SEP 22

Lincoln issues preliminary Emancipation Proclamation, freeing slaves in Confederate states.

OCT 3-4
Corinth (Mississippi) Gen. William Rosecrans defeats Gen. Earl Van Dorn.

NOTE: Battles are in black type, with flags indicating: Union victory ▦ Confederate victory ✕